WITHDRAWN

Baroness Scotland of Asthal

A PROFILE

Sue Adler
illustrated by Catherine Ward

Tamarind Ltd

OTHER BOOKS IN THE
Black Profiles Series

LORD JOHN TAYLOR OF WARWICK
BENJAMIN ZEPHANIAH
MALORIE BLACKMAN
DR SAMANTHA TROSS
JIM BRATHWAITE

Published by Tamarind Ltd 2001
PO Box 52, Northwood
Middlesex HA6 1UN, UK

Text © Sue Adler
Illustrations © Catherine Ward
Cover illustration © Gillian Hunt
Series editor: Simona Sideri

ISBN 1-870516-51-6

Printed in Singapore

Contents

CHAPTER ONE

Leaving for England

IN 1959, a lively four-year-old girl stood on tiptoe
on the deck of a gigantic ship. That little girl was
Patricia Scotland. Beside her stood her mother, five of
her six brothers and her three sisters. Around them
were hundreds of Dominicans ready to sail for
England. The ship's horn bellowed, telling everyone
on board and on the shore that they were finally on
the move.

"Let's wave good-bye to your cousins now," said
Patricia's mother, as she lifted up her youngest child.

The little girl peered over the railings of the ship and waved to her family and to Dominica, the small, mountainous Caribbean island that had been home to the Scotland family for years.

"You'll have to be very good, all of you. Stay close to me until I can find my way around this place," said their worried mother, looking at her nine children all ready to dash off in different directions.

Patricia, her mother, brothers and sisters were sailing over six thousand kilometres to join their father in England.

One year before, Mr Scotland had left Dominica on that same ship. "I'll send for you all just as soon as I can find a job and somewhere for us to live," he told his wife. He took their eldest son with him when he left.

The ship's horn bellowed again as they left the harbour. Two of the children cried, but they were all very excited about the adventures they would have on board. From one side of the ship they could see their beautiful tropical island disappearing into the distance. On the other side the sparkling blue sea glinted on and on to the horizon.

"Mum, when will we see Daddy?" Patricia asked.

"In sixteen days, God willing," her mother replied as she hugged her.

CHAPTER TWO

Life in Dominica

IN THE TOWN OF ST JOSEPH, in Dominica, where Patricia was born, Mr Scotland had worked as a policeman. He was well-liked and respected. If anyone had disputes or arguments with family, friends or neighbours, Mr Scotland would be asked to help them sort out the problems. He loved helping people, so when he left the police force, he became Parish Councillor for St Joseph. This meant he could work for all the people in the community.

The Scotland family had a good life in the Caribbean and a comfortable home. When he was young, Mr Scotland bought some land and Mrs Scotland inherited some from her parents.

The birth of Patricia, their tenth child, made the Scotlands seriously consider the future. They wanted all their children to have the very best education.

It was the 1950s and although schools were good on the small island, there was no university. The British, who ruled Dominica at that time, had made the local schools follow the British school system. This meant that anyone who wanted to go to

university was expected to go to England or America.

Mr and Mrs Scotland decided that the whole family should emigrate to England. That way they could be sure that all their children would have the benefits of higher education and the chance to have successful careers.

When Mr Scotland arrived in London, he was offered work as a carpenter and builder. This was not ideal but it meant the family could be together and the children could go to English schools. The family was reunited in a small house in Walthamstow, East London.

CHAPTER THREE

Chilly London

LIFE FOR THE SCOTLANDS in London was very different and sometimes difficult.

In Dominica it was always warm. In the rainy season, the sky clouded over and the rain came pouring down, but it was never long before the sun came out again.

In London, on a December afternoon, it was already dark by four o'clock. Quite often grey clouds hid the sunlight all day long and it was freezing.

Patricia remembered her favourite skirt, yellow with tiny red dots, that she had worn in Dominica. She looked down at her clumsy boots and remembered her soft brown sandals that showed her bare toes. She thought how it had taken just a few minutes to dress and run outside.

"Don't forget your gloves, Patricia!" her mother called as they both struggled into boots and thick coats. They were preparing to go out in the chilly streets to fetch the older children from school.

"I don't like wearing gloves, boots, and this scratchy coat. I feel all squashed up in these clothes," Patricia grumbled.

At first it was very different, the cold weather. The children thought it was very strange that they had to have a fire burning *inside* the house to keep them warm. Patricia enjoyed sitting by the fireplace watching the dancing orange flames and the sparks. She felt warm and cosy.

"Please, can I help shovel the coal on?" Patricia asked her older sister who looked after the fire.

"No, you're not old enough, Pat. And don't sit too close. You'll get horrible blotchy legs and I'll get into trouble if you get burnt!"

In the small house that the large family shared each child had a job to do. Sometimes they did it well – and sometimes they didn't.

Once when Patricia and her sister were supposed to be tidying their bedroom, they hid underneath a bed. A friend had given them a bag of sticky toffees. There weren't enough to share amongst them all, so the two children quickly ate the entire bag between them.

"I've got a tummy ache!" groaned Patricia.

"NO, you don't!" whispered her sister menacingly. "Tell you what, I'll teach you a nursery rhyme we learned at school. You'll feel better, ok?"

Sing a song of sixpence,
A pocket full of rye;
Four and twenty blackbirds,
Baked in a pie.

When the pie was opened,
The birds began to sing;
Was not that a dainty dish,
To set before the king?

"Better now?" asked her sister.

"NO!" groaned Patricia. "When I go to school, I'll learn better things than that. Cooked birds don't sing, silly. And my tummy still hurts!"

"Girls!" came Mrs Scotland's voice. "Have you finished tidying yet? I need you both to come here and try on your dresses."

The two girls scrambled out from under the bed. "Nearly ready!" they called and chased round the room, stuffing clothes into cupboards.

Downstairs in the living room, their mother had just finished sewing new dresses for the girls. Mrs Scotland never seemed to rest. She was on the go from morning to night, cooking, cleaning, washing, ironing, sewing, and then ferrying children to and from school every weekday. On Sunday it was church.

Patricia's older sisters and brothers all went to school not far from their home in East London.

Every day Patricia walked with her mum and the two younger children to meet the others at the school gate.

Every day Patricia asked her mother, "When can I go to school, Mum?"

"When you're five," her mother replied over and over again.

And then one day her mother said, "You'll be five soon, Pat!"

"Soon, I'll be a real school girl," said Patricia skipping along. "Soon, I'll read real books and have school friends."

She couldn't wait.

CHAPTER FOUR

Playtime

VERY SOON AFTER HER FIFTH BIRTHDAY, Patricia walked through the gates of Sir Thomas Scammel Primary School and waved goodbye to her mum. She loved being at school.

At home, her favourite game was to arrange everyone's toys in rows and pretend to be a teacher. Sometimes she managed to get her sisters and young brothers to sit in her pretend classroom.

"Today, we're going to learn the alphabet. Repeat after me A, B, C…" Patricia would rattle through from A to Z. "Now let's have a story."

One day as she read a story to her dolls, she suddenly stopped and spent some time looking at the pictures in the book.

"The children in this story look just like our dolls and not like me," said Patricia, pointing to the blue-eyed, fair-haired children in the pictures.

"No-one in the books in school ever looks like us, either," one of her older sisters said.

Just then, the girls heard a shout from one of their brothers. "Come on! Let's play outside. Race you to the pre-fabs!"

Patricia dropped her book and chased after the others, down the side of the house, across the garden, through the gate and onto a piece of open ground.

Here there was a row of little houses with tin roofs. They been built very quickly after World War II, when London had been badly bombed and many people lost their homes. By the 1960s the tinny little houses were deserted and shabby.

With two babies born in London, there were twelve children in the Scotland family now and those tiny buildings echoed with laughter and hammering footsteps. For the Scotland children, the pre-fabs were not depressing, dreary places. With great imagination they made them into fabulous palaces in a magical time.

"Let's pretend to be Extraordinary People!" Patricia, often the ring-leader, shouted. "Let's pretend we're on the moon, living in purple tents and eating mud cakes and drinking green lemonade."

Sometimes the games ran on and on and the children forgot the time.

Mrs Scotland knew exactly where to find them. She needed only to shout two words, **"Dinner time!"** and the gang would immediately return from the moon and race home.

"Hmm, it seems you didn't eat that much on the moon," Mrs Scotland smiled as she watched her children enjoy big helpings of rice and peas and Caribbean chicken stew.

Dinner was always lively, with fourteen people sitting around the table. Everyone talked about what sort of day they had had and there was lots of joking and laughter.

CHAPTER FIVE

Strong Faith

PATRICIA, LIKE HER MOTHER, sisters, brothers
and many people from Dominica, grew up a Roman
Catholic. Religion was part of everyday life in the
Scotland home. The family went to church every
Sunday, and prayed together every night.

One day, when she was seven years old, Patricia
went to hear a black evangelist preaching in a park
near Walthamstow. There was a huge crowd and the
preacher preached and prayed in a loud,
commanding voice. Behind him, a choir of women
dressed in neat white blouses and black skirts sang
hymns that made everyone want to clap and sing
along with them. And they did.

The service lasted for well over an hour. Near the
end the preacher said, "Brothers and sisters, anyone
who wants to receive the Holy Spirit should come
forward."

At first Patricia felt a bit giggly, but as the choir
continued to sing and clap their hands she suddenly
felt serious. She was overcome by a feeling of great
calm. She walked quietly to the front of the
congregation and stood. It was then that she realised

that her belief in God was real. That moment in her life remains vivid to this day.

Years later Patricia thought of joining the church and becoming a nun.

"Don't make any decisions for a while," advised both her parents. "Choose what you want to do in life very carefully."

CHAPTER SIX

Reading in the Dark

BEDTIME IN THE SCOTLAND HOUSEHOLD was strict. Lights-out for the younger children was at eight o'clock.

When Patricia was nine years old she was allowed to stay up an extra half hour. She begged to be allowed to stay up even later, to read.

"Off to bed, child. You need your sleep. You can finish your book tomorrow," her parents chorused.

Patricia shared a bedroom with the younger children, so she had to move quietly when she went up to bed. She regularly smuggled books and a torch under the thick blankets.

In her little den, she raced through dozens of library books. She read anything and everything, except horror stories.

Then around the time of her tenth birthday she discovered teenage novels. These books took quite a long time to finish so Patricia spent even more time reading under the covers.

One night she was in the middle of a very exciting book. Now and then she flashed her torch at the clock by her bed. All too soon, it was midnight. The house was deathly quiet.

"Oh no! It's so late!" she groaned. "But I've got to find out what happens next. Just one more chapter and I'll..."

She stretched her arm out from under the covers to point the torch at the clock for another look. The tinny little clock crashed to the floor. In the quiet room full of sleeping children the sound was very loud. She held her breath...

In a matter of seconds her father appeared at the door. "What's happening?" he asked as he hurried into the room. He saw the fallen clock and the torch lit up a guilty face.

"Patricia, you'll ruin your eyesight," he whispered. For a moment she thought he would be cross. "Come with me," he said and led her out of the room.

"My dear, we've tried everything, even taking out the bulb. But all you want to do is read. What are we going to do with you?"

Patricia smiled back. "Just one more chapter, Daddy," she said. "Please, I've nearly finished."

"Well, if you're going to read anyway, you might as well do it in good light and in comfort," he replied.

Delighted, Patricia followed him downstairs. Everyone else had gone to bed. She curled up on the biggest, softest chair with her book. Her father went to the kitchen and returned with two mugs of hot chocolate, and then he too sat down with his book.

CHAPTER SEVEN

Patricia the Dancer

AT SCHOOL Patricia was good at most subjects. She loved language. She loved people. She made many good friends.

Her primary school was not far from home, but when she went to secondary school she had to travel quite a long way. This happened because her father was determined to choose the best school for her and the one he eventually found was not near their home.

"I don't know anyone at that school, Daddy!" she complained. "None of the children from my primary school will be going there."

"Don't worry, my dear," he replied. "Your brother Barry will look after you. His school is not far away."

Barry was great. He didn't seem to mind, like so many growing lads, trailing his little sister behind him. He dropped her off at school every day and she waited for him at going home time.

The children were given bus fares daily for the journey. Sometimes they let the bus go and walked to and from school. They spent the bus fares on sticky jam doughnuts that they ate on the way home in the afternoon.

"My brothers are great, but at that time, Barry was my hero!" remembered Patricia many years later.

Patricia settled well in her new school. She was an excellent all-rounder. A good athlete, she was on many of her school's sports teams. She won the Waltham Forest 400m and in the same week played on the winning netball and rounders teams. On the academic side too, Patricia had an excellent record. English and history were her favourite subjects. Most of all, however, she loved to dance.

"How do you manage to learn so many steps so easily?" asked one teacher. "I'd like to know so that I can help the other children."

"I just listen to the music, Miss. And I let my body talk!" replied Patricia.

"Dance is my best thing, even better than running and netball," she told her sisters.

She often draped her mother's soft scarves around her and gave lively dancing performances in the bedroom.

Sometimes at home, their parents played old black vinyl records they'd brought to England from Dominica. They played calypso music and showed the children the lively Caribbean dance steps. Patricia only needed to see them make a couple of moves and she would follow them exactly, to the great delight of her parents and their friends.

In the ballet class, Patricia's teacher watched her closely. She enjoyed seeing the slender girl moving gracefully. "Now there's a girl who could become a professional dancer," she thought. The teacher was excited to have such a gifted girl in her class.

"Patricia, I'd like you to take the lead in the summer show," said the dance teacher one day. "It's quite a big part. Would you like that?" She went on, "You'll need a costume. A swirling cloak would be great."

Patricia smiled, "I'd love it! And there's no problem with the costume. My mother can easily make that. She sews all our clothes anyway."

The teacher had often admired the Scotland girls'

pretty clothes. She had never guessed that they were home-made.

The show was wonderful. It was a joint school play with the local boys' school. Patricia had three solo dances. Every time she appeared the audience were ecstatic. Patricia was a star. She dazzled everyone with her performance.

CHAPTER EIGHT

Listening to Her Parents

"MUM, DADDY, I think I could be a real dancer!"
Patricia said one day.

Her parents looked at each other. "What do you
mean by 'real'?" asked her mother quietly.

"When I've grown up. Dancing as my job. I **am**
good! All my teachers say so," Patricia replied.

Her father thought carefully before he spoke. "Patricia, you're a brilliant dancer. But you're also good at many other things and you're clever, just like your brothers and sisters."

"But I've been given prizes for dancing," argued Patricia.

"What do you mean you've been *given* prizes? You mean you won them," said her mother.

"Well," said Patricia, "when I won the first prize for English last week, the girl who came second was given it."

"What?" said both parents at once, horrified.

"Well," said Patricia, "my teacher said that I win prizes too easily without working hard, and the other girl deserved to win because she had worked harder than me."

"That's wrong and so unfair." Her father took a deep breath. "Patricia, are your teachers pushing you to be a dancer?" he asked. "Well, yes they are. Or maybe to do sport," she replied.

"You know, Patricia, some people think that all we Caribbean people can do is dance, sing and run. It is *so* wrong! You should be a doctor, not a dancer. Your brother wants to be a doctor. Tell you what, you study to be a doctor too, and then when your mother and I get old we can each have a doctor of our own to look after us," he said with a cheeky grin.

"A doctor? But I can't..."

Her mother interrupted gently, "There's no such word as *can't* in this family." She put an arm around Patricia. "You can always try. If you fail, well, that's no disgrace. The only disgrace is in **not** trying. Just always do your best, Patricia, and use the talents God has given you."

Patricia understood what her parents were telling her, but she felt sad.

CHAPTER NINE

Career Choices

LIFE AT HOME AND SCHOOL continued without major events for Patricia. Like many of her teenage friends, she worked in a supermarket on Saturdays. She felt quite grown-up and enjoyed the job.

At school, the time had come to choose what to study at college or what jobs to go for. Patricia and her classmates were sent to see the Careers teacher.

By then, Patricia had already made up her mind to go to university. All she needed was some advice from the Careers teacher to help her choose the best university and course for her.

She started by telling the teacher about her job at the supermarket. Patricia was just going to start explaining what she hoped to do in the future when the Careers teacher interrupted.

"That's excellent! If you continue to work hard in that supermarket, you can become a supervisor there. You shouldn't set your sights too high. Supermarket supervisor could be the best job for a girl like you!"

Patricia was confused. "What is she talking about? What does she mean by 'a girl like me'?" she wondered.

At home it was normal for the Scotland children to chat to each other and to their parents about the type of work they wanted to do. From her school reports, they all assumed, including Patricia, that she would go to university. After all, the reason they had travelled from Dominica was so that the children could get a good education.

Patricia went home and told her parents about her conversation with the Careers teacher. She was still shocked and surprised and needed her parents' support more than ever.

Her parents reminded her that she always had good marks and said she was quite right in believing that she could – and should – go to university.

"Don't worry about what the Careers teacher said," Patricia's mother told her. "She doesn't know everything!"

"What we really want is for all our children to be independent," said her father. "What do *you* want to do, Patricia?" he asked.

"I'm not really sure... I'm good at English!" replied Patricia.

"Well, maybe you could be a journalist," suggested her mother, "or a teacher... maybe."

Patricia had overheard her father saying to a friend that he really wanted some of his children to be scientists. He had said that he saw science and technology as the future, the direction the world was going in. "I want my children to be part of that," he had told his friend.

Patricia did not want to be a scientist, or a doctor, or a journalist, or a teacher. So she asked her parents to give her some time to think.

She was delighted when she passed three 'A' levels. She was only seventeen years old. That summer she stopped working in the supermarket and went for a job in a solicitor's office.

After working there for five or six weeks, she was sure that law was for her.

"I think I've decided," she said to her brother. "I want to do law."

"Why?" he asked.

"Well, because I can help people. I also like how the best lawyers perform. I really like that."

Patricia went to college in Chelmsford to do a law degree (LLB) in September 1973, aged eighteen. She had successfully completed it by the time she was twenty.

She loved being at university and made many friends. She worked hard and soon she was enjoying a life that combined her love of books and learning with her wish to help others.

She enjoyed having her own room in the halls of residence and being able to come and go as she pleased. At times the course work was difficult and Patricia spent many late nights at her desk. However, her life was wonderful. There were regular discos and parties, films and gigs. Many of the people she met at university were interesting and friendly and the three years passed very quickly.

CHAPTER TEN

Becoming a Lawyer

PATRICIA WANTED TO BE A BARRISTER. "I need an extra year to study with a master at one of the Inns of Court. Then I'll take the Bar exams and become a barrister, and I'll be able to work in the High Courts," she told her family.

It was not easy to find a place as a pupil with a practising barrister. She was bitterly disappointed when she was turned down time and time again. Many male barristers thought that it was not a good idea to take women on because they might soon leave to have children. But in the end, Patricia was finally offered a place at Middle Temple.

She was called to the Bar – becoming a fully-qualified barrister – in July 1977 when she was only twenty-two years old.

Patricia worked hard and her boss and the people around her at work started to take notice of her. She then won the Sir Winston Churchill prize, an award given to people most likely to succeed in their chosen career. Patricia was on her way to the top of her profession.

As a young black, female, award-winning lawyer, Patricia attracted a lot of attention from the newspapers. They were always on the lookout for an interesting story.

"I want to make a difference to people's lives and to be a voice for those people who are never heard. In my work I would do my best to see that justice is done and all people are treated truly equally in the eyes of the law," she told a reporter.

CHAPTER ELEVEN
Making a Difference

AFTER BECOMING A BARRISTER, Patricia returned to Dominica, where she was born. She had been away from the island for over twenty years and was very excited about going home.

The people were friendly and welcoming and she loved to sit in the bright sunshine and watch the rich green landscape and the magical sunsets.

She was tempted to stay and not return to England. In a telephone call to her parents she told her father, "I would like to settle here, Dad. I love it. It's beautiful and I'm so happy."

"Patricia, I think you should return. More black professional people are needed here in England to work and to make a difference in this country. Much work needs doing, especially with our young people and you are well placed here to do that. Maybe later in life you can return to the Caribbean to warm your old bones in the sun," he replied.

She thought about what her father had said and made up her mind. She had a wonderful holiday, and then returned to England to settle down to work.

Patricia had been brought up with ideas about equality and fairness for everyone. Her strong Christian faith and her studies had made her think deeply about the way the world worked. Like many black people of her time, Patricia was inspired by people who were brave enough to stand up and speak out for their ideas on equality and who worked to help others.

One of her role models is Mother Teresa, a nun who worked for many years among the poorest of the poor in the streets of Calcutta, in India. She also greatly admires the Reverend Martin Luther King, Jr, who worked tirelessly in America for equal rights for black people.

Over the years, Patricia's work has given her the chance to work for justice and fairness, in the law courts and on a number of government committees. She has combined the role of wife and mother of two sons with a successful career – an extremely difficult task.

CHAPTER TWELVE

Queen's Counsel

PATRICIA'S EXCELLENT WORK over a period of time as a barrister impressed many people, some of whom were in high positions. One of these people was the Lord Chancellor, Lord Mackay.

In 1991 he recommended that she should be appointed Queen's Counsel, or QC. This is a very senior position, given only to the top ten per cent of barristers.

Patricia was not sure she was ready to be a QC. "I'm only thirty-five. Can I do such a senior job?" she wondered.

Then she thought again of her mother's words all those years before. "There's no such thing as *can't*."

Patricia was the first black woman QC in England. She was also the youngest QC for more than two hundred years and the youngest person to achieve this honour in England since William Pitt the Younger became King's Counsel in 1780.

As a Queen's Counsel Patricia wears a silk gown in the courtroom, with a flat collar and long, hanging sleeves. King's and Queen's Counsels have worn gowns exactly like this since the early eighteenth century. Sometimes QCs are called 'silks' because of this clothing. For special official occasions, Patricia wears an elaborate wig, curled and made of horse-hair, which is very hot.

CHAPTER THIRTEEN

The House of Lords

IN NOVEMBER 1997, Patricia Janet Scotland QC was appointed by the new Labour government to the House of Lords. She was given the title Baroness Scotland of Asthal, in the County of Oxfordshire, for life. She was given this special honour because of the excellent work that she had done as a QC.

Patricia could never have become a baroness if various historical events had not happened.

The first took place in the year 1066, when William the Conqueror beat King Harold at the Battle of Hastings and took the English throne. William set up a Great Council of Lords to advise him, which over the centuries developed into the House of Lords as it exists today.

Another important date is 1958. This was when the Life Peerages Act was passed. Until that time only certain people could sit in the House of Lords. There were hereditary peers – people who had inherited land and titles from their parents. Important members of the church, such as archbishops and bishops, sat in the Lords, and also important judges.

So, in 1958, it was decided that the House of Lords needed to change. The Life Peerages Act meant that ordinary people could be given a title, such as Lord or Baroness, for their lifetime, as a reward for their hard work and service to the country. They would be able to sit in the House of Lords and be involved in governing the country.

In 1958, Patricia was just a toddler, living in Dominica. But if this Act had not been passed it would have been impossible for her to become a Baroness.

Yet another important date is 1963. This is when women were given the same rights in the House of Lords as men. Until that time women could not sit in the House of Lords.

Without these changes, Patricia could not have become a Baroness – the first black woman to do so.

Baroness Scotland has seen changes in the House of Lords, and as we begin the 21st century more changes are on the way. The government is still discussing who will sit in the House of Lords in the future and and how they will be chosen. It is an interesting time to be in the House and Baroness Scotland, with her legal training, is well-suited to considering the issues involved.

CHAPTER FOURTEEN

A Very Busy Life

IN JULY 1999, Baroness Scotland's life changed again. She became the British Government's first ever black woman minister – yet another first for her, and the country. The Prime Minister, Tony Blair, appointed her Under Secretary of State for Foreign and Commonwealth Affairs.

Patricia has responsibility for the Caribbean and North America. She also works with the British Council and is responsible for Information with the BBC World Service. One of her duties is to answer Foreign Office questions in the House of Lords. She

has achieved her wish to help those who cannot make themselves heard and is their voice in Government.

As a government minister she works harder than ever. Quite often, her day starts at eight-thirty in the morning and goes on until two the next morning – seventeen and a half hours later.

"I meet many important people in this new job. Just one example – I recently had a meeting with the Prime Minister of Antigua and Barbuda. That day, we discussed a problem with British nuclear waste that is shipped through the Caribbean. Nuclear products are extremely dangerous and their movement around the world has to be monitored very carefully as it can endanger vast areas of land and sea. We also discussed the crisis caused by the volcano on the

island of Montserrat. It's good to talk, especially when one can really help," she said.

Patricia works hard to make the United Kingdom a fairer place for us all. She is a QC, a Baroness and a Government Minister. She has worked with the Millennium Commission and the Commission for Racial Equality. She is also a member of many legal committees.

She is a Master of the Middle Temple – the first black woman to have been made a Master. She is also a member of the Bar of Antigua and the Commonwealth of Dominica, a member of the Lawyer's Christian Fellowship, a Deputy High Court Judge of the Family Division. She works with many, many other groups – and she's a mum!

Patricia says, "I sometimes think that it was a total miracle that I have got to where I am. I am troubled by people saying that I am an exception. I had an ordinary enough childhood. My advantage is my excellent family. There are hundreds of young children out there with superb talents – with the right help and support, they can and *will* succeed. I had my family's support at all times. I am truly blessed."